Table of Contents

Embroidering Eyes on Amigurumi

Skill Level
Beginner

Materials
- Medium (worsted) weight yarn:
  5 feet black
  1 foot white
- Tapestry needle

4 MEDIUM

Pattern Notes
Weave in loose ends as work progresses.

If you're looking for a baby-safe alternative to plastic safety eyes, this tutorial will teach you how to embroider eyes.

Right and left are as you are looking at work throughout. For example, if you are looking at front of the face, right eye is on right as you see it.

Work embroidery after the head is stuffed and closed.

Special Technique
End: End each part by bringing needle out at same st as beg tail. Cut yarn leaving 4-inch tail. Tie tails tog and tuck into Head.

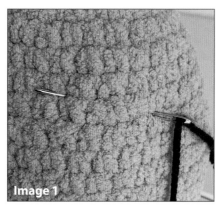

Image 1

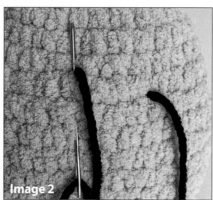

Image 2

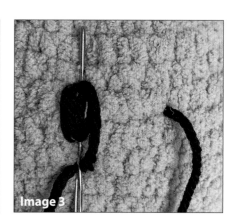

Image 3

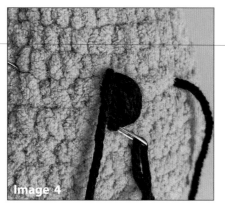

Image 4

Image 5

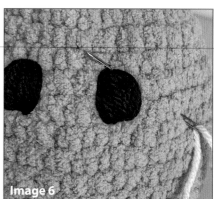

Image 6

Embroidery

Eye

With 4 feet of black and tapestry needle, insert needle into right side of head and bring it out where top of eye will be, leaving a 6-inch tail *(see image 1)*.

Insert needle back into head 2 rnds below *(bottom of eye)* and bring it out at the top of the eye *(1 wrap—see image 2)*. Continue wrapping several times, not overlapping, but also leaving no sp in between wraps and alternating sides each wrap, to create the round shape *(see image 3)*.

When right eye has the desired fullness and round shape, use same yarn to create left eye in the same manner, bringing yarn loosely through head to beg *(see image 4)*. When left eye is complete, work **end** *(see Special Technique and image 5)*.

Eye Highlight

With 12 inches of white and tapestry needle, insert needle into right side of head and bring it out at top center of eye *(top of first wrap—see image 6)*, leaving a 4-inch tail. Insert needle below bottom center of right eye *(first highlight made—see image 7)*, ensure highlights are snug against edge of eye. Bring needle through Head and out at bottom center of left eye. Insert needle at top center of left eye *(2nd highlight made)* and bring it out at top center of right eye then insert it in center of eye *(sparkle made—see image 8)*. Bring needle out at top center of left eye then insert it in center of same eye *(2nd sparkle made)* and work end *(see image 9)*.

Eyelashes

With rem 1 foot of black and tapestry needle, insert needle into right side of head, bring it out at top left corner of right eye, just left of white sparkle *(see image 10)*, insert needle halfway down on right side of right eye and 1 st to the right *(see image 11)*, bring needle out halfway down on left side of left eye and 1 st to the left, then insert it in right corner of left eye just right of white sparkle and work end *(see image 12)*. ●

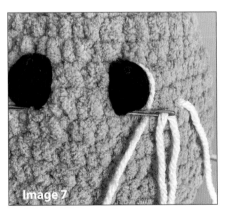
Image 7

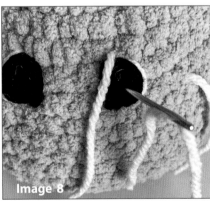
Image 8

Image 9

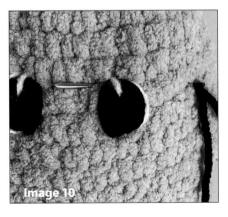
Image 10

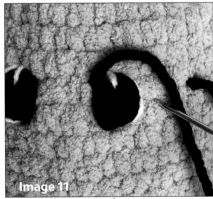
Image 11

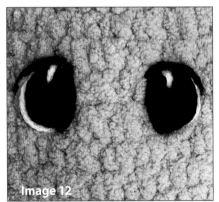
Image 12

Henry the Horse

Skill Level
Intermediate

Finished Measurement
27 inches long from ears to toes

Materials
- Bernat Blanket Yarn super bulky (super chunky) weight polyester yarn (10½ oz/220 yds/300g per skein):
    - 1 skein each #010014 sand, #010029 taupe and #010040 coal
    - Small amount #010986 birch
- Bernat Super Value medium (worsted) weight acrylic yarn (7 oz/440 yds/197g per skein):
    - 1 yd each #07391 white and #07421 black (for eyes)
- Size K/10½/6.5mm crochet hook or size needed to obtain gauge
- Tapestry needle
- Fiberfill
- 20mm safety eyes: 2
- Stitch marker

Gauge
With super bulky yarn: 10 sc = 4 inches; 5 sc rnds = 4 inches

About Henry

In the charming town of Beaufort, South Carolina, lives a spirited horse named Henry who revels in the simple pleasures of life. Every morning, after his long drink from the water pail, he lies down in the sun-drenched pasture to bask in the golden rays for hours. Then it's time for lunch with his equine besties—Carla, Eunice and Sullivan—under a shady tree. Apples, carrots and hay always hit the spot for these four. They spend the afternoon on a trail ride in the woods and work up quite an appetite. By nightfall, Henry is cozily nestled in his stall with a full belly of oats and ready for some z's—standing up, of course, dreaming of another perfect day in the beautiful low country.

Pattern Notes

Head, Ear and Leg begin with a slip ring. If preferred, instead of a slip ring, chain 3 and slip stitch into first chain to form beginning ring.

Do not join or turn at end of round unless indicated. Mark first stitch of round and move marker up with each round.

Join with slip stitch as indicated unless otherwise stated.

Weave in loose ends as work progresses unless otherwise stated.

Right and left are as you are looking at work throughout. For example, if you are looking at front of face, right eye is on right as you see it *(which would be Henry's left eye).*

Sew pieces together as indicated with tapestry needle and matching yarn using photos as a guide. Use long tails for sewing wherever possible.

This is a snuggler design, meaning Body will not be stuffed.

To embroider eyes in lieu of using safety eyes, see Embroidering Eyes on Amigurumi tutorial on page 2.

Chain-2 at beginning of round does not count as a stitch unless otherwise stated.

Special Stitch

Bobble: Yo, insert hook in indicated st, yo, pull up a lp, yo and draw through 2 lps *(2 lps on hook)*, [yo, insert hook in same st, yo, pull up a lp, yo and draw through 2 lps] 3 times *(5 lps on hook)*, yo, draw through all 5 lps.

Henry the Horse

Head

Rnd 1: With birch, form a **slip ring** *(see illustration and Pattern Notes)*, 8 sc in ring, pull tail to close ring, **do not join** *(see Pattern Notes). (8 sts)*

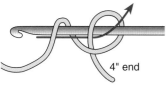

4" end

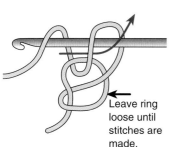

Leave ring loose until stitches are made.

Slip Ring

Rnd 2: 2 sc in each st around. *(16 sts)*

Rnd 3: [2 sc in next st, sc in next st] around. *(24 sts)*

Rnds 4 & 5: Sc in each st around. *(24 sts)*

Rnd 6: Sc in next 8 sts, **bobble** (see Special Stitch) in next st, sc in next 6 sts, bobble in next st, sc in last 8 sts, **changing to sand** (see illustration) in last st. (2 bobbles, 22 sc)

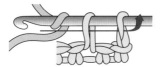

Single Crochet Color Change

Rnds 7–13: Sc in each st around. (24 sts)

Rnd 14: Sc in next 13 sts, change to birch, sc in next 2 sts, change to sand, sc in next 9 sts. (24 sts)

Rnd 15: [2 sc in next st, sc in next 2 sts] 4 times, change to birch, sc in next 4 sts, change to sand, sc in next 2 sts, [2 sc in next st, sc in next 2 sts] twice. (30 sts)

Rnds 16 & 17: Sc in next 17 sts, change to birch, sc in next 3 sts, change to sand, sc in next 10 sts. (30 sts)

Rnd 18: Sc in next 18 sts, change to birch, sc in next 2 sts, change to sand, sc in next 10 sts. (30 sts)

Snap in **safety eyes** (see Pattern Notes) between rnds 15 and 16 with 3 birch sts between eyes.

Beg to stuff with fiberfill and continue stuffing as work progresses.

Rnd 19: Sc in next 19 sts, change to birch, sc in next st, change to sand, sc in next 10 sts. (30 sts)

Rnd 20: [2 sc in next st, sc in next 4 sts] around. (36 sts)

Rnds 21–23: Sc in each st around. (36 sts)

Rnd 24: [**Sc dec** (see Stitch Guide) in next 2 sts, sc in next 4 sts] around. (30 sts)

Rnd 25: [Sc dec in next 2 sts, sc in next 3 sts] around. (24 sts)

Rnd 26: [Sc dec in next 2 sts, sc in next 2 sts] around. (18 sts)

Rnd 27: [Sc dec in next 2 sts, sc in next st] around. (12 sts)

Rnd 28: [Sc dec in next 2 sts] 6 times. (6 sts)

Fasten off, leaving an 8-inch tail. Weave tail through rem 6 sts and pull tightly to close.

Eye Highlights

Part 1

With a 12-inch length of white and tapestry needle, insert needle into **right** (see Pattern Notes) side of head and bring it out just above top right corner of right eye, leaving a 4-inch tail (see image).

Insert needle below bottom center of right eye (first highlight made—see image), bring it through Head and out at top left corner of left eye. Insert needle at bottom center of left eye (2nd highlight made) and bring it out at same st as beg tail (see image). Cut yarn leaving a 4-inch tail. Tie tails tog and tuck into Head.

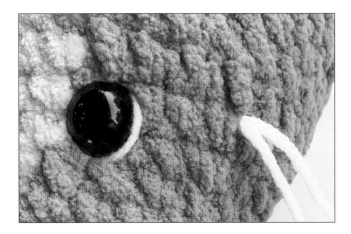

Bring needle back out at same st as beg tail. Tie tails tog and tuck into Head.

Part 2

With a 16-inch length of black and tapestry needle, insert needle into right side of Head and bring it out at center top of right eye, leaving a 4-inch tail. Insert needle into Head halfway down right side of same eye and 1 st to right *(highlight made—see image)*. Bring needle out at center top of left eye, insert needle halfway down left side of same eye and 1 st to left *(2nd highlight made)*. Do not fasten off.

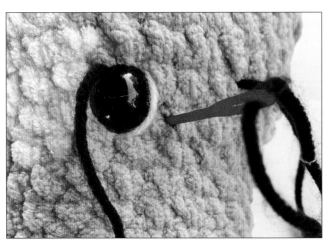

Eyebrows

Bring needle out between rnds 17 and 18 in line with left side of left eye, insert needle 1 row up and 1 st to the right between rnds 18 and 19 *(eyebrow made)*, bring needle up between rnds 18 and 19 in line with left side of right eye, insert needle 1 row down and 1 st to the right between rnds 17 and 18 *(2nd eyebrow made—see image)*.

Ear
Make 2.

Rnd 1: With sand, form a slip ring, 6 sc in ring, pull tail to close ring. *(6 sts)*

Rnd 2: 2 sc in each st around. *(12 sts)*

Rnd 3: Sc in each st around. *(12 sts)*

Rnd 4: [2 sc in next st, sc in next st] around. *(18 sts)*

Rnd 5: Sc in each st around. *(18 sts)*

Rnd 6: [2 sc in next st, sc in next 2 sts] around. *(24 sts)*

Rnd 7: Sc in each st around. *(24 sts)*

Rnd 8: [Sc dec in next 2 sts, sc in next 2 sts] around. *(18 sts)*

Rnds 9 & 10: Sc in each st around. *(18 sts)*

Fasten off, leaving an 8-inch tail. Pinch bottom of ear tog to create concave shape. Using tail and tapestry needle, sew pinched end closed and sew to Head between rnds 22 and 26 with 6 sts showing between ears.

Body
Note: *Body is crocheted directly onto bottom of Head.*

Rnd 1: Turn head upside down, facing muzzle away from you, insert hook under center bottom st on rnd 24, yo with sand and pull yarn through *(see image)*, **ch 2** *(see Pattern Notes)*, working under posts of sts and creating an oval shape, 12 dc around bottom of Head *(see image)*, **join** *(see Pattern Notes)* in beg ch-2. *(12 sts)*

Rnds 2 & 3: Ch 2, dc in each st around, join in beg ch-2. *(12 sts)*

Rnd 4: Ch 2, 2 dc in first st, dc in next st, [2 dc in next st, dc in next st] around, join in beg ch-2. *(18 sts)*

Rnd 5: Ch 2, dc in each st around, join in beg ch-2. *(18 sts)*

Rnd 6: Ch 2, 2 dc in first st, dc in next 2 sts, [2 dc in next st, dc in next 2 sts] around, join in beg ch-2. *(24 sts)*

Rnd 7: Rep rnd 5.

Rnd 8: Ch 2, 2 dc in first st, dc in next 3 sts, [2 dc in next st, dc in next 3 sts] around, join in beg ch-2. *(30 sts)*

Rnd 9: Ch 2, 2 dc in first st, dc in next 4 sts, [2 dc in next st, dc in next 4 sts] around, join in beg ch-2. *(36 sts)*

Rnd 10: Ch 2, 2 dc in first st, dc in next 5 sts, [2 dc in next st, dc in next 5 sts] around, join in beg ch-2. *(42 sts)*

Rnd 11: Ch 2, 2 dc in first st, dc in next 6 sts, [2 dc in next st, dc in next 6 sts] around, join in beg ch-2. *(48 sts)*

Rnds 12 & 13: Rep rnd 5.

Rnd 14: Ch 2, **dc dec** *(see Stitch Guide)* in first 2 sts, dc in next 6 sts, [dc dec in next 2 sts, dc in next 6 sts] around, join in beg ch-2. *(42 sts)*

Rnd 15: Rep rnd 5.

Rnd 16: Ch 2, dc dec in first 2 sts, dc in next 5 sts, [dc dec in next 2 sts, dc in next 5 sts] around, join in beg ch-2. *(36 sts)*

Rnd 17: Rep rnd 5.

Rnd 18: Ch 2, dc dec in first 2 sts, dc in next 4 sts, [dc dec in next 2 sts, dc in next 4 sts] around, join in beg ch-2. *(30 sts)*

Rnd 19: Ch 2, dc dec in first 2 sts, dc in next 3 sts, [dc dec in next 2 sts, dc in next 3 sts] around, join in beg ch-2. *(24 sts)*

Row 20 (seam): Press row flat, ch 1, working through both layers at the same time, sc in each pair of sts across. Fasten off. *(12 sts)*

Leg
Make 4.

Rnd 1: With coal, form a slip ring, 8 sc in ring, pull tail to close ring, do not join. *(8 sts)*

Rnd 2: 2 sc in each st around. *(16 sts)*

Rnd 3: [2 sc in first st, sc in next st] around. *(24 sts)*

Rnd 4: Sc in **horizontal bar** *(see illustration)* of each st around. *(24 sts)*

**Horizontal Bar of
Single Crochet**

Rnd 5: Sc in each st around. *(24 sts)*

Rnd 6: [Sc dec in next 2 sts, sc in next st] around, changing to sand in last st. Fasten off coal. *(16 sts)*

Rnds 7 & 8: Rep rnd 5.

Beg to stuff with fiberfill and continue stuffing as work progresses.

Rnd 9: [Sc dec in next 2 sts, sc in next 2 sts] around. *(12 sts)*

Rnds 10–14: Rep rnd 5. *(12 sts)*

Rnd 15: [Sc dec in next 2 sts, sc in next 2 sts] around. *(9 sts)*

Rnd 16: Rep rnd 5. *(9 sts)*

Rnd 17: [Sc dec in next 2 sts, sc in next st] around. *(6 sts)*

Rnd 18: Rep rnd 5. *(6 sts)*

Fasten off, leaving an 8-inch tail.

Use tapestry needle to sew 2 front Legs onto Body between rnds 5 and 6, sew 2 back Legs onto Body between rnds 19 and 20 *(see image)*.

Mane

Work around sts as for beg of Body.

With top of Head facing you, insert hook under st in rnd 22 even with right eye, yo with taupe and pull yarn through, *ch 16, insert hook in next st to the left, yo and pull through, sl st into previous ch-16 lp, rep back and forth across forehead toward back of Head until 10 ch-16 lps have been made to create bangs. Move down head and neck rep this process *(see image)*, ending on rnd 4 of Body, but inc chs to 30, or make lps as long or short as desired. Fasten off.

Tail

Starting on rnd 18 at center back of Body, work in the same manner as Mane, making 45-st chs instead of 16-st chs. Add lps to desired fullness. ●

Birdie the Bear

Skill Level
Confident Beginner

Finished Measurement
19½ inches long from ears to toes

Materials
- Bernat Blanket Yarn super bulky (super chunky) weight polyester yarn (10½ oz/220 yds/300g per skein):
  - 1 skein each #10986 birch and #10928 deep fuchsia
  - Small amount #10955 white
- Bernat Super Value medium (worsted) weight acrylic yarn (7 oz/440 yds/197g per skein):
  - 1 yd each #07391 white and #07421 black (for eyes)
- Size K/10½/6.5mm crochet hook or size needed to obtain gauge
- Size L/11/8mm crochet hook (for Head Wrap)
- Tapestry needle
- Fiberfill
- 20mm safety eyes: 2
- Stitch marker

Gauge
With super bulky yarn and smaller hook: 10 dc = 4 inches; 5 dc rnds = 4 inches

About Birdie
Birdie is a true girlie girl at heart. She adores all things fashionably fuchsia. Birdie resides in quaint Watkinsville, Georgia, where she is often spotted in her favorite fuchsia dress and head wrap. She loves organizing tea parties for her best friends, Poppy, Marissa and MaryAnne, and showcasing her stylish ensembles. Her radiant personality and impeccable taste make her a fashion icon in Watkinsville and admired by all her friends.

Pattern Notes
All pieces except Body and Head Wrap begin with a slip ring. If preferred, instead of a slip ring, chain 3 and slip stitch into first chain to form beginning ring.

Do not join or turn at end of round unless indicated. Mark first stitch of round and move marker up with each round.

Join with a slip stitch as indicated unless otherwise stated.

Weave in ends as work progresses unless otherwise stated.

Right and left are as you are looking at work throughout. For example, if you are looking at front of the face, right eye is on right as you see it *(which would be Birdie's left eye).*

Sew pieces together as indicated with tapestry needle and matching yarn using photos as a guide. Use long tails for sewing wherever possible.

This is a snuggler design, meaning Body will not be stuffed.

For embroidered eyes in lieu of safety eyes, see Embroidering Eyes on Amigurumi tutorial on page 2.

Chain-2 at beginning of round does not count as a stitch unless otherwise stated.

Special Stitch

Color change join: Insert hook in top of ch-2, yo with next color, drop old color, pull lp through st and lp on hook *(as a sl st).*

Birdie the Bear

Snout

Rnd 1: With super bulky white and smaller hook, form a **slip ring** *(see illustration and Pattern Notes)*, 8 sc in ring, pull tail to close ring, **do not join** *(see Pattern Notes).* *(8 sts)*

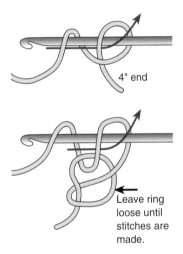

4" end

Leave ring loose until stitches are made.

Slip Ring

Rnd 2: 2 sc in each st around. *(16 sts)*

Rnd 3: [2 sc in next st, sc in next st] around. *(24 sts)*

Rnd 4: [2 sc in next st, sc in next 2 sts] around. *(32 sts)*

Rnd 5: Sc in each st around. *(32 sts)*

Rnd 6: [**Sc dec** *(see Stitch Guide)* in next 2 sts, sc in next 2 sts] around. *(24 sts)*

Rnd 7: Sc in each st around, **changing to birch** *(see illustration)* in last st. Fasten off white. *(24 sts)*

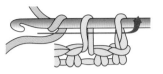

Single Crochet Color Change

Rnd 8: Sc in each st around. *(24 sts)*

Fasten off, leaving a 16-inch tail. Stuff with fiberfill.

Head

Rnd 1: With birch and smaller hook, form a slip ring, 8 sc in ring, pull tail to close ring, do not join. *(8 sts)*

Rnd 2: 2 sc in each st around. *(16 sts)*

Rnd 3: [2 sc in next st, sc in next st] around. *(24 sts)*

Rnd 4: [2 sc in next st, sc in next 2 sts] around. *(32 sts)*

Rnd 5: [2 sc in next st, sc in next 3 sts] around. *(40 sts)*

Rnds 6–18: Sc in each st around. *(40 sts)*

Snap in **safety eyes** *(see Pattern Notes)* between rnds 11 and 12 with 7 sts between eyes.

Beg to stuff with fiberfill and continue stuffing as work progresses.

Rnd 19: [Sc dec in next 2 sts, sc in next 3 sts] around. *(32 sts)*

Rnd 20: [Sc dec in next 2 sts, sc in next 2 sts] around. *(24 sts)*

Rnd 21: [Sc dec in next 2 sts, sc in next st] around. *(16 sts)*

Rnd 22: [Sc dec in next 2 sts] around. *(8 sts)*

Fasten off, leaving an 8-inch tail. Weave tail through rem 8 sts and pull tightly to close.

Finishing & Assembly

Gently press top and bottom of Snout tog to make a slight oval shape *(see image)*. Keeping Snout in oval shape, place top edge between rnds 12 and 13 and bottom edge between rnds 19 and 20 and sew in place.

Nose

Thread a 5-foot length of deep fuchsia onto tapestry needle. Insert needle in **right** *(see Pattern Notes)* side of snout and bring it out in center of slip ring *(see image)*, then *insert needle between rnds 4 and 5 at center top of Snout and back out at center of slip ring, rep from * changing insertion point at top of snout by 1 st over twice on each side of center to have 5 strands of yarn over front of Snout *(see image)*, creating nose.

Continue to wrap in the same manner, alternating through same 5 sts at top of Snout until nose is full, then bring needle out in same sp where it first entered Snout. Tie beg and end tails tog and tuck into Head.

Eye Highlights

With 12 inches of worsted-weight white and tapestry needle, insert needle in right side of head and bring it out at right side of right eye, leaving a 4-inch tail. Insert needle at bottom left corner of right eye *(highlight made—see image)* and bring it out at bottom right corner of left eye, insert needle at center left edge of left eye *(2nd highlight made)* and bring it out at same st as beg tail. Cut yarn leaving a 4-inch tail. Tie tails tog and tuck into Head.

With 18 inches of black and tapestry needle, insert needle in right side of head, coming out at top left corner of right eye, leaving a 4-inch tail. Insert needle 1 st away from right side of same eye *(highlight made—see image)*, bring it out at top right corner of left eye. Insert needle 1 st away from left side of same eye *(2nd highlight made)*. Do not fasten off.

Eyebrows

Bring needle out between rnds 8 and 9 and in line with left side of left eye. Insert needle 2 sts to the right and between rnds 7 and 8 *(eyebrow made)*, bring it up between rnds 7 and 8 in line with left side of right eye. Insert needle 2 sts to the right between rnds 8 and 9 and bring it out in same st as beg tail. Cut yarn leaving a 4-inch tail. Tie tails tog and tuck into Head.

Ear
Make 2.

Rnd 1: With birch and smaller hook, form a slip ring, 8 sc in ring, pull tail to close ring, do not join. *(8 sts)*

Rnd 2: 2 sc in each st around. *(16 sts)*

Rnd 3: [2 sc in next st, sc in next st] around. *(24 sts)*

Rnd 4: Sc in each st around. *(24 sts)*

Rnd 5: [Sc dec in next 2 sts, sc in next st] around. *(16 sts)*

Rnd 6: Rep rnd 4. *(16 sts)*

Rnd 7: [Sc dec in next 2 sts, sc in next 2 sts] around. *(12 sts)*

Fasten off, leaving a 12-inch tail and sew at an angle onto either side of Head between rnds 4 and 10.

Body

Rnd 1: With birch, smaller hook and leaving a 16-inch tail, form a slip ring, **ch 2** *(see Pattern Notes)*, 12 dc in ring, pull tail to close ring, **join** *(see Pattern Notes)* in beg ch-2. *(12 sts)*

Use needle to pull long tail through center of ring. Tail will be used later to sew Body onto Head.

Rnd 2: Ch 2, 2 dc in each st around, **color change join** *(see Special Stitch)* to deep fuchsia. Fasten off birch. *(24 sts)*

Rnd 3: Ch 2, dc in each st around, join in beg ch-2. *(24 sts)*

Rnd 4: Ch 2, 2 dc in first st, dc in next st, [2 dc in next st, dc in next st] around, join in beg ch-2. *(36 sts)*

Rnds 5–7: Rep rnd 3. *(36 sts)*

Rnd 8: Ch 2, 2 dc in first st, dc in next 3 sts, [2 dc in next st, dc in next 3 sts] around, join in beg ch-2. *(45 sts)*

Rnds 9 & 10: Rep rnd 3. *(45 sts)*

Rnd 11: Ch 2, dc in each st around, color change join to birch. *(45 sts)*

Fasten off deep fuchsia.

Rnd 12: Rep rnd 3. *(45 sts)*

Rnd 13: Ch 2, **dc dec** *(see Stitch Guide)* in first 2 sts, dc in next st, [dc dec in next 2 sts, dc in next st] around, join in beg ch-2. *(30 sts)*

Row 14 (seam): Press row flat, ch 1, working through both layers, sc in each pair of sts across. Fasten off. *(15 sts)*

With beg tail, sew Body onto bottom of Head between rnds 2 and 3 of Body so birch on Head blends with birch on Body *(see image)*.

Arm
Make 2.

Rnd 1: With birch and smaller hook, form a slip ring, 8 sc in ring, pull tail to close ring, do not join. *(8 sts)*

Rnd 2: 2 sc in each st around. *(16 sts)*

Rnds 3–7: Sc in each st around. *(16 sts)*

Rnd 8: [Sc dec in next 2 sts, sc in next 2 sts] around. *(12 sts)*

Rnds 9 & 10: Sc in each st around. *(12 sts)*

Beg stuffing with fiberfill and continue stuffing as work progresses.

Rnd 11: [Sc dec in next 2 sts, sc in next 2 sts] around. *(9 sts)*

Rnds 12 & 13: Sc in each st around. *(9 sts)*

Rnd 14: [Sc dec in next 2 sts, sc in next st] around. *(6 sts)*

Rnd 15: Sc in each st around, changing to deep fuchsia in last st. *(6 sts)*

Rnd 16: Sc in each st around. *(6 sts)*

Fasten off, leaving an 8-inch tail and sew Arms on either side of Body where Head and Body meet.

Dress

Rnd 1: With deep fuchsia and smaller hook, place bear with back facing up, insert hook around post of st on center back of body on rnd 11 *(see image)*, ch 2, working around posts of sts on rnd 11, 2 sc in same st as join, sc in next 2 sts, [2 sc in next st, sc in next 2 sts] around, join in beg ch-2. *(60 sts)*

Rnds 2 & 3: Ch 2, dc in each st around, join in beg ch-2. *(60 sts)*

Rnd 4: Sl st in each st around. Fasten off. *(60 sts)*

Leg
Make 2.

Rnd 1: With birch and smaller hook, form a slip ring, 8 sc in ring, pull tail to close ring, do not join. *(8 sts)*

Rnd 2: 2 sc in each st around. *(16 sts)*

Rnds 3–8: Sc in each st around. *(16 sts)*

Rnd 9: [Sc dec in next 2 sts, sc in next 2 sts] around. *(12 sts)*

Rnds 10 & 11: Sc in each st around. *(12 sts)*

Fasten off, leaving a 12-inch tail. Stuff with fiberfill and sew onto 2 bottom corners of Body.

Tail

Rnd 1: With birch and smaller hook, form a slip ring, 8 sc in ring, pull tail to close ring, do not join. *(8 sts)*

Rnd 2: 2 sc in each st around. *(16 sts)*

Rnds 3–5: Sc in each st around. *(16 sts)*

Rnd 6: [Sc dec in next 2 sts, sc in next 2 sts] around. *(12 sts)*

Fasten off, leaving an 8-inch tail. Stuff with fiberfill and sew onto back of Body between rnds 12 and 14.

Head Wrap

With deep fuchsia and larger hook, ch 80, dc in 3rd ch from hook and each rem ch. Fasten off. *(78 sts)*

Place Head Wrap around top part of head, tie in a bow in front. ●

Darlene the Duck

Skill Level
Confident Beginner

Finished Measurement
26 inches long from head feathers to end of feet

Materials
- Bernat Blanket Yarn super bulky (super chunky) weight polyester yarn (10½ oz/220 yds/300g per skein):
    - 1 skein each #10918 sunsoaked, #10630 pumpkin spice and #10136 sailor's delight
- Bernat Super Value medium (worsted) weight acrylic yarn (7 oz/440 yds/197g per skein):
    - 1 yd each #07391 white and #07421 black (for eyes)
- Size K/10½/6.5mm crochet hook or size needed to obtain gauge
- Tapestry needle
- Fiberfill
- 20mm safety eyes: 2
- Stitch marker

Gauge
With super bulky yarn: 10 dc = 4 inches; 5 dc rnds = 4 inches

Pattern Notes
All pieces except Body and Scarf begin with a slip ring. If preferred, instead of a slip ring, chain 3 and slip stitch into first chain to form beginning ring.

Do not join or turn at end of rounds unless indicated. Mark first stitch of round and move marker up with each round.

Join with a slip stitch as indicated unless otherwise stated.

Weave in ends as work progresses unless otherwise stated.

Right and left are as you are looking at work throughout. For example, if you are looking at front of the face, right eye is on right as you see it (which would be Darlene's left eye).

Sew pieces together as indicated with tapestry needle and matching yarn and using photos as a guide. Use long tails for sewing wherever possible.

This is a snuggler design, meaning Body will not be stuffed.

For embroidered eyes in lieu of safety eyes, see Embroidering Eyes on Amigurumi tutorial on page 2.

Chain-2 at beginning of round does not count as a stitch unless otherwise stated.

About Darlene

Darlene the Duck is quite the sensation in her charming town of Norcross, Georgia. She is known not only for her fun array of scarves, but also for her extraordinary piano skills. Wrapped in her beautiful scarf, she waddles elegantly to the old piano in the corner of the local café every afternoon. Her personality and music fill the air with warmth and joy because seriously—who doesn't want to watch a duck play the piano? Her best friends, Gregg, Stephen and Myrtle, come to the café on the weekends to watch her play, all wearing scarves in support of Darlene, of course.

Darlene the Duck

Bill

Rnd 1: With pumpkin spice, form a **slip ring** (see illustration and Pattern Notes), 6 sc in ring, pull tail to close ring, **do not join** (see Pattern Notes). (6 sts)

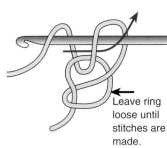

Slip Ring

Rnd 2: Sc in each st around. (6 sts)

Rnd 3: [2 sc in next st, sc in next st] around. (9 sts)

Rnd 4: Sc in each st around. (9 sts)

Rnd 5: [2 sc in next st, sc in next 2 sts] around. (12 sts)

Rnd 6: [2 sc in next st, sc in next st] around. (18 sts)

Rnd 7: Sc in next 7 sts, 2 sc in next 4 sts, sc in next 7 sts. (22 sts)

Rnd 8: Sc in next 10 sts, 2 sc in next 2 sts, sc in next 10 sts, **changing to sunsoaked** (see illustration) in last st. (24 sts)

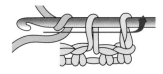

Single Crochet Color Change

Rnd 9: Working in **back lps** (see Stitch Guide), sl st in each st around. (24 sts)

Fasten off, leaving a 16-inch tail.

Stuff with fiberfill.

Head

Rnd 1: With sunsoaked, form a slip ring, 8 sc in ring, pull tail to close ring, do not join. (8 sts)

Rnd 2: 2 sc in each st around. (16 sts)

Rnd 3: [2 sc in next st, sc in next st] around. (24 sts)

Rnds 4 & 5: Sc in each st around. (24 sts)

Rnd 6: [2 sc in next st, sc in next 2 sts] around. (32 sts)

Rnds 7 & 8: Sc in each st around. (32 sts)

Rnd 9: [2 sc in next st, sc in next 3 sts] around. (40 sts)

Rnds 10 & 11: Sc in each st around. (40 sts)

Rnd 12: [2 sc in next st, sc in next 4 sts] around. (48 sts)

Rnds 13–20: Sc in each st around. (48 sts)

Snap in **safety eyes** (see Pattern Notes) between rnds 11 and 12 with 7 sts between eyes.

Beg to stuff with fiberfill and continue stuffing as work progresses.

Rnd 21: [Sc dec (see Stitch Guide) in next 2 sts, sc in next 4 sts] around. (40 sts)

Rnd 22: [Sc dec in next 2 sts, sc in next 3 sts] around. (32 sts)

Rnd 23: [Sc dec in next 2 sts, sc in next 2 sts] around. (24 sts)

Rnd 24: [Sc dec in next 2 sts, sc in next st] around. (16 sts)

Rnd 25: [Sc dec in next 2 sts] 8 times. (8 sts)

Fasten off, leaving an 8-inch tail. Weave tail through rem 8 sts and pull tightly to close.

Sew Bill onto Head. Matching top of Bill to rnd 11 of Head and bottom of Bill to rnd 19.

Head Feathers

Cut 4 8-inch strands of sunsoaked and thread 1 strand onto tapestry needle. Insert needle between rnds 1 and 2 of Head and bring out in center of slip ring. Tie a knot twice to secure *(see image)*. Rep for rem 3 strands, trim to 1½ inches long.

Eye Highlights

With a 12-inch length of white and tapestry needle, insert needle into **right** *(see Pattern Notes)* side of head and bring it out just above top right corner of right eye, leaving a 4-inch tail *(see image)*. Insert needle below bottom center of right eye *(first highlight made—see image)*, bring it through Head and out at top left corner of left eye. Insert needle at bottom center of left eye *(2nd highlight made)* and bring it out at same st as beg tail *(see image)*. Cut yarn leaving a 4-inch tail. Tie tails tog and tuck into Head.

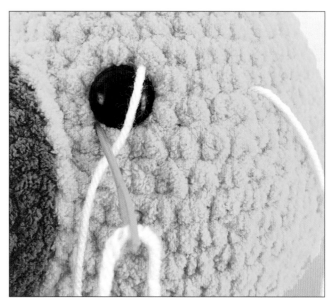

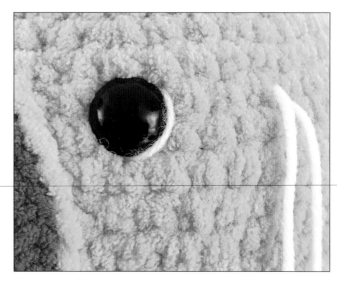

Eyebrows

With a 12-inch length of black and tapestry needle, insert needle into right side of Head and bring it out between rnds 9 and 10 in line with right side of right eye, leaving a 4-inch tail *(see image)*, insert needle 2 sts to the left between rnds 7 and 8 *(eyebrow made)*, bring needle up between rnds 7 and 8 in line with right side of left eye, insert needle 2 sts to the left between rnds 9 and 10 *(2nd eyebrow made)*.

Bring needle back out at same st as beg tail. Tie tails tog and tuck into Head.

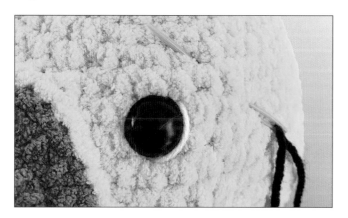

Body

Note: *Body is crocheted directly onto bottom of Head.*

Rnd 1: Turn Head upside down with Bill facing away from you, insert hook between rnds 24 and 25 of Head, yo with sunsoaked and pull yarn through *(see image)*, **ch 2** *(see Pattern Notes)*, working under posts of sts between rnds 24 and 25 and creating an oval shape, 12 dc around bottom of Head *(see image)*, **join** *(see Pattern Notes)* in beg ch-2. *(12 sts)*

Rnd 2: Ch 2, 2 dc in first st, dc in next st, [2 dc in next st, dc in next st] around, join in beg ch-2. *(18 sts)*

Rnd 3: Ch 2, dc in each st around, join in beg ch-2. *(18 sts)*

Rnd 4: Ch 2, 2 dc in first st, dc in next 2 sts, [2 dc in next st, dc in next 2 sts] around, join in beg ch-2. *(24 sts)*

Rnd 5: Rep rnd 3. *(24 sts)*

Rnd 6: Ch 2, 2 dc in first st, dc in next 3 sts, [2 dc in next st, dc in next 3 sts] around, join in beg ch-2. *(30 sts)*

Rnd 7: Rep rnd 3. *(30 sts)*

Rnd 8: Ch 2, 2 dc in first st, dc in next 4 sts, [2 dc in next st, dc in next 4 sts] around, join in beg ch-2. *(36 sts)*

Rnd 9: Rep rnd 3. *(36 sts)*

Rnd 10: Ch 2, 2 dc in first st, dc in next 5 sts, [2 dc in next st, dc in next 5 sts] around, join in beg ch-2. *(42 sts)*

Rnds 11–14: Rep rnd 3. *(42 sts)*

Rnd 15: Ch 2, **dc dec** *(see Stitch Guide)* in first 2 sts, dc in next 5 sts, [dc dec in next 2 sts, dc in next 5 sts] around, join in beg ch-2. *(36 sts)*

Rnd 16: Ch 2, dc dec in first 2 sts, dc in next 4 sts, [dc dec in next 2 sts, dc in next 4 sts] around, join in beg ch-2. *(30 sts)*

Rnd 17: Ch 2, dc dec in first 2 sts, dc in next 3 sts, [dc dec in next 2 sts, dc in next 3 sts] around, join in beg ch-2. *(24 sts)*

Row 18 (seam): Press row flat, ch 1, working through both layers, sc in each pair of sts across *(see image)*. Fasten off. *(12 sts)*

Wing
Make 2.

Rnd 1: With sunsoaked, form a slip ring, 6 sc in ring, pull tail to close ring, do not join. *(6 sts)*

Rnd 2: Sc in each st around. *(6 sts)*

Rnd 3: 2 sc in each st around. *(12 sts)*

Rnd 4: Rep rnd 2. *(12 sts)*

Rnd 5: [2 sc in next st, sc in next st] around. *(18 sts)*

Rnd 6: Rep rnd 2. *(18 sts)*

Rnd 7: [2 sc in next st, sc in next 2 sts] around. *(24 sts)*

Rnd 8: Rep rnd 2. *(24 sts)*

Rnd 9: [2 sc in next st, sc in next 3 sts] around. *(30 sts)*

Rnds 10 & 11: Rep rnd 2. *(30 sts)*

Rnd 12: [Sc dec in next 2 sts, sc in next 3 sts] around. *(24 sts)*

Rnd 13: Rep rnd 2. *(24 sts)*

Rnd 14: [Sc dec in next 2 sts, sc in next 2 sts] around. *(18 sts)*

Rnd 15: Rep rnd 2. *(18 sts)*

Rnd 16: [Sc dec in next 2 sts, sc in next st] around. *(12 sts)*

Rnd 17: Rep rnd 2. *(12 sts)*

Rnd 18: [Sc dec in next 2 sts] around. *(6 sts)*

Fasten off, leaving an 8-inch tail. With tail, sew Wings over rnd 3 on both sides of Body.

Foot
Make 2.

Rnd 1: With sunsoaked and leaving an 8-inch tail for sewing, form a slip ring, 6 sc in ring, changing to pumpkin spice in last st, pull tail to close ring, do not join. *(6 sts)*

Rnd 2: Sc in each st around. *(6 sts)*

Use tapestry needle to pull beg tail through ring.

Rnds 3–5: Rep rnd 2. *(6 sts)*

Rnd 6: 2 sc in each st around. *(12 sts)*

Rnd 7: Rep rnd 2. *(12 sts)*

Rnd 8: [2 sc in next st, sc in next st] around. *(18 sts)*

Rnds 9–11: Rep rnd 2. *(18 sts)*

Row 12 (seam): Press row flat, ch 1, working through both layers, sc in each pair of sts across. *(9 sts)*

Sew each Foot onto bottom corners of Body.

Tail

Rnd 1: With sunsoaked, form a slip ring, 6 sc in ring, pull tail to close ring, do not join. *(6 sts)*

Rnd 2: Sc in each st around. *(6 sts)*

Rnd 3: 2 sc in each st around. *(12 sts)*

Rnd 4: Rep rnd 2. *(12 sts)*

Fasten off, leaving an 8-inch tail. With tail, sew onto back of Body between rnds 14 and 17.

Scarf

Rnd 1: With sailor's delight, ch 7, dc in 3rd ch from hook and each rem ch across, turn. *(5 sts)*

Rnds 2–52: Ch 2, dc in each st across, turn. Fasten off. *(5 sts)* ●

Davis the Dachshund

Skill Level
Intermediate

Finished Measurement
23 inches long

Materials
- Bernat Blanket Yarn super bulky (super chunky) weight polyester yarn (10½ oz/220 yds/300g per skein):
    - 1 skein each #10029 taupe, #10014 sand and #10630 pumpkin spice
    - 5 yds #10040 coal
- Bernat Super Value medium (worsted) weight acrylic yarn (7 oz/440 yds/197g per skein):
    - 1 yd each #07391 white and #07421 black (for eyes)
- Size K/10½/6.5mm crochet hook or size needed to obtain gauge
- Tapestry needle
- Fiberfill
- 20mm safety eyes: 2
- Stitch marker

Gauge
With super bulky yarn: 7 sc = 4 inches; 7 sc rnds = 4 inches

Pattern Notes
All pieces except Body and Vest begin with a slip ring. If preferred, instead of a slip ring, chain 3 and slip stitch into first chain to form beginning ring.

Do not join or turn at end of rounds unless indicated. Mark first stitch of round and move marker up with each round.

Join with a slip stitch as indicated unless otherwise stated.

Weave in ends as work progresses.

Change colors as indicated by using new color to complete last pull-through step of last stitch of previous color.

Right and left are as you are looking at work throughout. For example, if you are looking at front of face, right eye is on right as you see it (which would be Davis' left eye).

Sew pieces together as indicated with tapestry needle and matching yarn and using photos as a guide. Use long tails for sewing wherever possible.

This is a snuggler design, meaning Body will not be stuffed.

To embroider eyes in lieu of using safety eyes, see Embroidering Eyes on Amigurumi tutorial on page 2.

Chain-2 at beginning of round does not count as a stitch unless otherwise stated.

About Davis

Davis the Dachshund is the epitome of canine cool. He struts around his small town of North Augusta, South Carolina, with a snazzy vest that makes him the center of attention. Davis' fun-loving personality is as vibrant as his fashion sense. His best friends—Eric, Simona and Cita—love grabbing a bite to eat with Davis on the weekends. Their favorite spot is the local hot dog joint, of course! Davis is a true trendsetter with a zest for life and appetite for fun.

Davis the Dachshund

Snout

Rnd 1 (RS): With sand, form a **slip ring** (*see illustration and Pattern Notes*), 8 sc in ring, pull tail to close ring, **do not join** (*see Pattern Notes*). (*8 sts*)

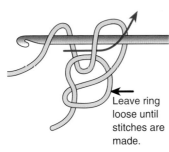

Slip Ring

Rnd 2: 2 sc in each st around. (*16 sts*)

Rnds 3–5: Sc in each st around. (*16 sts*)

Rnd 6: [2 sc in next st, sc in next 3 sts] around. (*20 sts*)

Rnds 7–9: Sc in each st around. (*20 sts*)

Rnd 10: Rep rnd 6. (*25 sts*)

Rnd 11: Change to taupe (*see Pattern Notes*), sc in each st around. (*25 sts*)

Fasten off, leaving a 16-inch tail. Stuff Snout with fiberfill and set aside.

Head

Rnd 1 (RS): With taupe, form a slip ring, 8 sc in ring, pull tail to close ring. (*8 sts*)

Rnd 2: 2 sc in each st around. (*16 sts*)

Rnd 3: [2 sc in next st, sc in next st] around. (*24 sts*)

Rnd 4: [2 sc in next st, sc in next 2 sts] around. (*32 sts*)

Rnds 5 & 6: Sc in each st around. (*32 sts*)

Rnd 7: [2 sc in next st, sc in next 3 sts] around. (*40 sts*)

Rnds 8–15: Sc in each st around. (*40 sts*)

Snap in **safety eyes** (*see Pattern Notes*) between rnds 9 and 10, with 6 sts between eyes.

Begin stuffing Head with fiberfill and continue stuffing as work progresses.

Rnd 16: [**Sc dec** *(see Stitch Guide)* in next 2 sts, sc in next 3 sts] around. *(32 sts)*

Rnd 17: Sc in each st around. *(32 sts)*

Rnd 18: [Sc dec in next 2 sts, sc in next 2 sts] around. *(24 sts)*

Rnd 19: [Sc dec in next 2 sts, sc in next st] around. *(16 sts)*

Rnd 20: Sc dec in next 2 sts around. *(8 sts)*

Fasten off, leaving a 16-inch tail.

Nose

Sew *(see Pattern Notes)* Snout to front of Head, centered between and 1 rnd below Eyes.

With coal and tapestry needle, insert needle into **right** *(see Pattern Notes)* side of Snout and bring it out in center of beg ring, leaving about a 5-inch tail. Insert needle between rnds 2 and 3 at top of Snout and come out at center of ring. Sew 2 more vertical sts on each side of this center st in the same manner but inserting needle 2 sts to left or right of previous vertical st each time *(see image)*. These 5 sts define edges of Nose.

Continue sewing vertical sts in the same manner, placing new sts between first 5 vertical sts until nose is full *(see image)*. On last st, bring yarn out in same st as beg tail. Cut yarn leaving a 5-inch tail. Tie tails tog and tuck into Snout.

Ear
Make 2.

Rnd 1 (RS): With taupe, form a slip ring, 8 sc in ring. *(8 sts)*

Rnd 2: Sc in each st around. *(8 sts)*

Rnd 3: 2 sc in each st around. *(16 sts)*

Rnds 4 & 5: Sc in each st around. *(16 sts)*

Rnd 6: [2 sc in next st, sc in next st] around. *(24 sts)*

Rnds 7–10: Sc in each st around. *(24 sts)*

Rnd 11: [2 sc in next st, sc in next 2 sts] around. *(32 sts)*

Rnd 12: Sc in each st around. *(32 sts)*

Rnd 13: [Sc dec in next 2 sts, sc in next 2 sts] around. *(24 sts)*

Rnd 14: Sc in each st around. *(24 sts)*

Rnd 15: [Sc dec in next 2 sts, sc in next st] around. *(16 sts)*

Rnds 16 & 17: Sc in each st around. *(16 sts)*

Rnd 18: [Sc dec in next 2 sts, sc in next 2 sts] around. *(12 sts)*

Rnds 19–22: Sc in each st around. *(12 sts)*

Rnd 23: [Sc dec in next 2 sts, sc in next 2 sts] around. *(9 sts)*

Rnd 24: Sc in each st around. *(9 sts)*

Rnd 25: [Sc dec in next 2 sts, sc in next st] around. *(6 sts)*

Rnds 26 & 27: Sc in each st around. *(6 sts)*

Fasten off, leaving a 12-inch tail for sewing.

Sew Ear to side of Head on rnd 4.

Eyebrows

With black and tapestry needle, insert needle into side of Head and bring it out 2 rnds above right side of right eye, leaving a 5-inch tail. Insert needle 2 sts to left and 1 rnd above where it came out *(first eyebrow made—see image)* and bring it out 6 sts further to left on same row. Insert needle 2 sts further to left and 1 rnd below where it came out *(2nd eyebrow made)*, and bring end out through same st as beg tail. Cut yarn leaving a 5-inch tail. Tie tails tog and tuck into Head.

Eye Highlights

With white and tapestry needle, insert needle into right side of Head and bring it out at top right corner of right eye, leaving a 5-inch tail. Insert needle at bottom center of right eye *(first highlight made)* and bring it out at top right corner of left eye. Insert needle at bottom center of left eye *(2nd highlight made)* and bring it out at same st as beg tail. Cut yarn leaving a 5-inch tail. Tie tails tog and tuck into Head.

Body

Rnd 1 (RS): Turn Head upside down with Nose facing away from you. Join taupe with sl st between any sts of rnds 19 and 20, ch 2, placing all sts between rnds 19 and 20, 16 dc evenly sp around Head *(see image)*, **join** *(see Pattern Notes)* in beg ch-2. *(16 sts)*

Rnd 2: Ch 2, 2 dc in first st, dc in next 3 sts, [2 dc in next st, dc in next 3 sts] around, join in beg ch-2. *(20 sts)*

Rnd 3: Ch 2, dc in each st around, join in beg ch-2. *(20 sts)*

Rnd 4: Ch 2, 2 dc in first st, dc in next 3 sts, [2 dc in next st, dc in next 3 sts] around, join in beg ch-2. *(25 sts)*

Rnd 5: Ch 2, dc in each st around, join in beg ch-2. *(25 sts)*

Rnd 6: Ch 2, 2 dc in first st, dc in next 4 sts, [2 dc in next st, dc in next 4 sts] around, join in beg ch-2. *(30 sts)*

Rnds 7–13: Ch 2, dc in each st around, join in beg ch-2. *(30 sts)*

Rnd 14: Ch 2, **dc dec** *(see Stitch Guide)* in first 2 sts, sc in next 3 sts, [dc dec in next 2 sts, sc in next 3 sts] around. *(24 sts)*

Rnd 15: Ch 2, dc in each st around, join in beg ch-2. *(24 sts)*

Rnd 16: Ch 2, dc dec in first 2 sts, sc in next 2 sts, [dc dec in next 2 sts, sc in next 2 sts] around. *(18 sts)*

Rnd 17: Ch 2, dc in each st around, join in beg ch-2. *(18 sts)*

Row 18 (seam): Press row flat so that front and back of Body line up with front and back of Head, ch 1, working through both layers, sc in each pair of sts across. Fasten off. *(9 sts)*

Front Paw & Leg
Make 2.

Front Paw
Rnd 1 (RS): With sand, form a slip ring, 8 sc in ring. *(8 sts)*

Rnd 2: 2 sc in each st around. *(16 sts)*

Rnd 3: Sc in each st around. Change to taupe. *(16 sts)*

Front Leg
Rnds 4 & 5: Sc in each st around. *(16 sts)*

Rnd 6: [Sc dec in next 2 sts, sc in next 2 sts] around. *(12 sts)*

Rnd 7: Sc in each st around. *(12 sts)*

Rnd 8: [Sc dec in next 2 sts, sc in next 2 sts] around. *(9 sts)*

Rnd 9: Sc in each st around. *(9 sts)*

Stuff with fiberfill up to rnd 7 only.

Rnd 10: [Sc dec in next 2 sts, sc in next st] around. *(6 sts)*

Rnd 11: Sc in each st around. *(6 sts)*

Fasten off, leaving an 8-inch tail for sewing.

Paw Print

Toes
Using taupe and tapestry needle, insert needle into side of Leg between rnds 3 and 4, bring needle out at any st between rnds 2 and 3 of Paw, insert needle between rnds 1 and 2 to make a vertical line, working in same 2 sts, *bring needle out between rnds 2 and 3, insert needle between rnds 1 and 2; rep from * 3 more times for Center Toe.

Working 2 sts to left of Center Toe, rep from * 5 times for Left Toe. Working 2 sts to right of Center Toe, rep from * 5 times for Right Toe, bring yarn out at center of Paw.

Paw Pad
Insert needles between rnds 1 and 2 at bottom of Paw *(directly below Center Toe)*, bring needle out 1 st to right of center of Paw, insert needle in same st at bottom of Paw, bring needle out 1 st to left of center of Paw, insert needle in same st at bottom of paw.

These 3 sts define edges of Paw Pad *(see image)*.

Continue sewing sts in the same manner, placing new sts between first 3 vertical sts until Paw Pad is full. On last st, bring yarn out in same st as beg tail. Cut yarn leaving a 5-inch tail. Tie tails tog and tuck into Leg.

Attach Leg to Body
Sew Front Leg to side of Body between rnds 1 and 2.

Back Paw & Leg
Make 2.

Back Paw
Work as for Front Paw.

Back Leg
Rnds 4–9: Work as for rnds 4–9 of Front Leg.

Stuff with fiberfill up to rnd 7 only.

Fasten off, leaving an 8-inch tail for sewing.

Paw Print
Work as for Front Leg.

Attach Leg to Body
Sew Back Leg to bottom of Body at rnd 18.

Tail
Rnd 1 (RS): With taupe, form a slip ring, 6 sc in ring. *(6 sts)*

Rnd 2: Sc in each st around. *(6 sts)*

Rnd 3: [2 sc in next st, sc in next 2 sts] around. *(8 sts)*

Rnds 4–6: Sc in each st around. *(8 sts)*

Rnd 7: [2 sc in next st, sc in next 3 sts] around. *(10 sts)*

Rnds 8–12: Sc in each st around. *(10 sts)*

Stuff with fiberfill.

Fasten off, leaving an 8-inch tail for sewing.

Sew Tail to back of Body between Rnds 15 and 16.

Vest
Row 1 (RS): With pumpkin spice, ch 21, sc in 2nd ch from hook and each ch across, turn. *(20 sts)*

Row 2: Ch 1, 2 sc in first st, sc in next 2 sts, ch 6, sk next 6 sts, sc in next 2 sts, ch 6, sk next 6 sts, sc in next 2 sts, 2 sc in last st, turn. *(10 sts, 2 ch-6 sps)*

Row 3: Ch 1, sc in each st and 6 sc in each ch-6 sp across, turn. *(22 sts)*

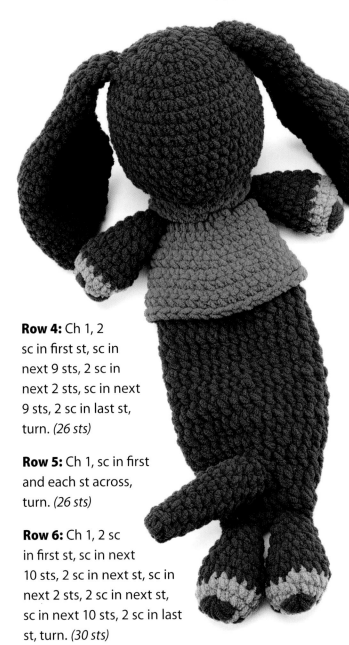

Row 4: Ch 1, 2 sc in first st, sc in next 9 sts, 2 sc in next 2 sts, sc in next 9 sts, 2 sc in last st, turn. *(26 sts)*

Row 5: Ch 1, sc in first and each st across, turn. *(26 sts)*

Row 6: Ch 1, 2 sc in first st, sc in next 10 sts, 2 sc in next st, sc in next 2 sts, 2 sc in next st, sc in next 10 sts, 2 sc in last st, turn. *(30 sts)*

Row 7: Ch 1, sc in each st across, turn. *(30 sts)*

Row 8: Ch 1, 2 sc in first st, sc in next 11 sts, 2 sc in next st, sc in next 4 sts, 2 sc in next st, sc in next 11 sts, 2 sc in last st, turn. *(34 sts)*

Rows 9 & 10: Ch 1, sc in first and each st across, turn. *(34 sts)*

Row 11: Ch 1, sc in first and each st across, do not turn. *(34 sts)*

Edging rnd (RS): Ch 1, sl st evenly sp around outside edge of Vest, fasten off.

With row 1 of Vest at top, place Front Legs through ch-6 sps in Vest. ●

Derrick the Dinosaur

Skill Level
Intermediate

Finished Measurement
21 inches long (including cap)

Materials
- Bernat Blanket Yarn super bulky (super chunky) weight polyester yarn (10½ oz/220 yds/300g per skein):
  1 skein each #10855 smoky green, #10920 deep sea and #10040 coal
  Small amount #10918 sunsoaked
- Bernat Super Value medium (worsted) weight acrylic yarn (7 oz/440 yds/197g per skein):
  1 yd each #07391 white and #07421 black (for eyes)
- Size K/10½/6.5mm crochet hook or size needed to obtain gauge
- Tapestry needle
- Fiberfill
- 20mm safety eyes: 2
- Stitch marker

Gauge
With super bulky yarn: 10 dc = 4 inches;
5 dc rnds = 4 inches

Pattern Notes
All pieces except Body and Cap begin with a slip ring. If preferred, instead of a slip ring, chain 3 and slip stitch into first chain to form beginning ring.

Do not join or turn at end of rounds unless indicated. Mark first stitch of round and move marker up with each round.

Join with a slip stitch as indicated unless otherwise stated.

Weave in ends as work progresses.

Right and left are as you are looking at work throughout. For example, if you are looking at front

of the face, right eye is on right as you see it *(which would be Derrick's left eye)*.

Sew pieces together as indicated with tapestry needle and matching yarn using photos as a guide. Use long tails for sewing wherever possible.

This is a snuggler design, meaning Body will not be stuffed.

To embroider eyes in lieu of using safety eyes, see Embroidering Eyes on Amigurumi tutorial on page 2.

Chain-2 at beginning of round does not count as a stitch unless otherwise stated.

Special Stitch

Bobble: Yo, insert hook in indicated st, yo and pull up a lp, yo and draw through 2 lps *(2 lps on hook)*,

[yo, insert hook in same st, yo and pull up a lp, yo and draw through 2 lps] 3 times *(5 lps on hook)*, yo and draw through all 5 lps.

About Derrick

Derrick's big day has finally arrived! He worked so hard to earn his degree from the local community college in Radford, Virginia, and his scales are shimmering with excitement. Derrick is standing tall among his classmates because he overcame unique challenges as a dinosaur in a human-centric world. Now, he is ready to clutch his degree, and he feels a profound sense of accomplishment and pride. As he walks across the stage, his mighty roar echoes through the crowd. He sees his best friend, Gerald, cheering him on in the crowd and begins to tear up. This is not just the end of his academic journey, but the beginning of a very promising future. Congratulations, Derrick!

Derrick the Dinosaur

Head

Rnd 1 (RS): With deep sea, form a **slip ring** *(see illustration and Pattern Notes)*, 8 sc in ring, **do not join** *(see Pattern Notes)*. *(8 sts)*

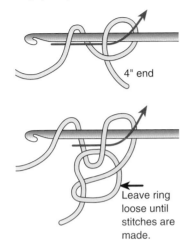

Slip Ring

Rnd 2: 2 sc in each st around. *(16 sts)*

Rnd 3: [2 sc in next st, sc in next st] around. *(24 sts)*

Rnd 4: [2 sc in next st, sc in next 2 sts] around. *(32 sts)*

Rnd 5: [2 sc in next st, sc in next 3 sts] around. *(40 sts)*

Rnd 6: Sc in first 14 sts, **bobble** *(see Special Stitch)* in next st, sc in next 8 sts, bobble in next st, sc in next 16 sts. *(38 sc, 2 bobble Nostrils)*

Rnds 7–9: Sc in each st around. *(40 sts)*

Rnd 10: [**Sc dec** *(see Stitch Guide)* in next 2 sts, sc in next 3 sts] around. *(32 sts)*

Rnds 11–15: Sc in each st around. *(32 sts)*

Rnd 16: [Sc dec in next 2 sts, sc in next 6 sts] around. *(28 sts)*

Rnds 17 & 18: Sc in each st around. *(28 sts)*

Rnd 19: [Sc dec in next 2 sts, sc in next 5 sts] around. *(24 sts)*

Rnds 20–23: Sc in each st around. *(24 sts)*

Note: *Rnd 1 is front of Head/tip of Snout; Nostrils are at top of Head.*

Snap in **safety eyes** *(see Pattern Notes)* between rnds 15 and 16, with 2 sts between eyes and centered across Nostrils.

Begin stuffing Head with fiberfill and continue stuffing as work progresses.

Rnd 24: [Sc dec in next 2 sts, sc in next 2 sts] around. *(18 sts)*

Rnd 25: [Sc dec in next 2 sts, sc in next st] around. *(12 sts)*

Rnd 26: [Sc dec in next 2 sts] around. *(6 sts)*

Fasten off, leaving a 12-inch tail for sewing. Sew hole closed with tail.

Body

Turn Head upside down with eyes at bottom and tip of Snout facing away from you. **Join** *(see Pattern Notes)* deep sea between rnds 22 and 23, 3 sts to **right** *(see Pattern Notes)* of center st *(see image)*.

Rnd 1 (RS): Ch 2 (see Pattern Notes), working in an oval shape (see image), dc in same st as join, dc 1 rnd directly above last dc made, [dc 1 rnd above and 1 st to left of last dc made] twice, [dc in next st on same rnd (between rnds 19 and 20)] twice, [dc 1 rnd below and 1 st to left of last dc made] twice, dc 1 rnd directly below last dc made, [dc 1 rnd below and 1 st to right of last dc made] twice, [dc in next st on same rnd (between rnds 22 and 23)] twice, dc 1 rnd above and 1 st to right of last dc made, join to beg ch-2. (14 sts)

Rnd 2: Ch 2, dc in each st around, join in beg ch-2. (14 sts)

Rnd 3: Ch 2, 2 dc in first st, dc in next 2 sts, [2 dc in next st, dc in next 2 sts] around to last 2 sts, dc in last 2 sts, join in beg ch-2. (18 sts)

Rnd 4: Ch 2, dc in each st around. (18 sts)

Rnd 5: Ch 2, 2 dc in first st, dc in next 2 sts, [2 dc in next st, dc in next 2 sts] around, join in beg ch-2. (24 sts)

Rnd 6: Ch 2, 2 dc in first st, dc in next 3 sts, [2 dc in first st, dc in next 3 sts] around, join in beg ch-2. (30 sts)

Rnd 7: Ch 2, dc in each st around. (30 sts)

Rnd 8: Ch 2, 2 dc in first st, dc in next 4 sts, [2 dc in next st, dc in next 4 sts] around, join in beg ch-2. (36 sts)

Rnd 9: Ch 2, 2 dc in first st, dc in next 5 sts, [2 dc in next st, dc in next 5 sts] around, join in beg ch-2. (42 sts)

Rnds 10–14: Ch 2, dc in each st around. (42 sts)

Rnd 15: Ch 2, **dc dec** (see Stitch Guide) in first 2 sts, dc in next 5 sts, [dc dec in next 2 sts, dc in next 5 sts] around, join in beg ch-2. (36 sts)

Rnd 16: Ch 2, dc dec in first 2 sts, dc in next 4 sts, [dc dec in next 2 sts, dc in next 4 sts] around, join in beg ch-2. (30 sts)

Rnd 17: Ch 2, dc dec in first 2 sts, dc in next 3 sts, [dc dec in next 2 sts, dc in next 3 sts] around, join in beg ch-2. (24 sts)

Rnd 18: Ch 2, dc in each st around. (24 sts)

Do not stuff Body (see Pattern Notes).

Fasten off, leaving a 16-inch tail for sewing. Sew Body closed.

Eyebrows

With black and tapestry needle, insert needle into side of Head and bring it out above right side of right eye between rnds 17 and 18, leaving a 5-inch tail. Insert needle 2 sts to left and between rnds 19 and 20 (first eyebrow made) and bring out 2 sts further to left on same row (see image). Insert needle 2 sts further to left and between rnds 17 and 18 (2nd eyebrow made) and bring end out through same st as beg tail. Cut yarn leaving a 5-inch tail. Tie tails tog and tuck into Head.

Eye Highlights

With white and tapestry needle, insert needle into right side of Head and bring it out at top right corner of right eye, leaving a 5-inch tail. Insert needle at bottom center of right eye *(first highlight made)* and bring it out at bottom center of left eye *(see image)*. Insert needle at top left corner of left eye *(2nd highlight made)* and bring it out at same st as beg tail. Cut yarn leaving a 5-inch tail. Tie tails tog and tuck into Head.

Arm

Make 2.

Rnd 1 (RS): With deep sea, form a slip ring, 8 sc in ring. *(8 sts)*

Rnd 2: 2 sc in each st around. *(16 sts)*

Rnds 3–5: Sc in each st around. *(16 sts)*

Rnd 6: [Sc dec in next 2 sts, sc in next 2 sts] around. *(16 sts)*

Rnd 7: Sc in each st around. *(16 sts)*

Rnd 8: [Sc dec in next 2 sts, sc in next 2 sts] around. *(12 sts)*

Rnd 9: [Sc dec in next 2 sts, sc in next 2 sts] around. *(9 sts)*

Stuff with fiberfill through rnd 9 only. Do not continue stuffing as work progresses.

Rnd 10: [Sc dec in next 2 sts, sc in next st] around. *(6 sts)*

Rnd 11: Sc in each st around. *(6 sts)*

Fasten off, leaving an 8-inch tail for sewing. Sew Arm to side of Body at rnd 4.

Leg

Make 2.

Rnd 1 (RS): With deep sea, form a slip ring, 8 sc in ring. *(8 sts)*

Rnd 2: 2 sc in each st around. *(16 sts)*

Rnd 3: [2 sc in next st, sc in next st] around. *(24 sts)*

Rnds 4 & 5: Sc in each st around. *(24 sts)*

Rnd 6: [Sc dec in next 2 sts, sc in next 2 sts] around. *(18 sts)*

Rnds 7 & 8: Sc in each st around. *(18 sts)*

Rnd 9: [Sc dec in next 2 sts, sc in next st] around. *(12 sts)*

Stuff with fiberfill through rnd 9 only. Do not continue stuffing as work progresses.

Rnds 10 & 11: Sc in each st around. *(12 sts)*

Fasten off, leaving an 8-inch tail for sewing. Sew Leg to bottom of Body at rnd 4.

Tail

Rnd 1 (RS): With deep sea, form a slip ring, 6 sc in ring. *(6 sts)*

Rnd 2: Sc in each st around. *(6 sts)*

Rnd 3: [2 sc in next st, sc in next st] around. *(9 sts)*

Rnds 4–6: Sc in each st around. *(9 sts)*

Rnd 7: [2 sc in next st, sc in next 2 sts] around. *(12 sts)*

Rnds 8 & 9: Sc in each st around. *(12 sts)*

Rnd 10: [2 sc in next st, sc in next 2 sts] around. *(16 sts)*

Rnd 11: Sc in each st around. *(16 sts)*

Rnd 12: [2 sc in next st, sc in next 3 sts] around. *(20 sts)*

Rnd 13: Sc in each st around. *(20 sts)*

Rnd 14: [2 sc in next st, sc in next 4 sts] around. *(24 sts)*

Rnd 15: Sc in each st around. *(24 sts)*

Rnd 16: [2 sc in next st, sc in next 3 sts] around. *(30 sts)*

Fasten off, leaving a 24-inch tail for sewing. Stuff with fiberfill. Sew Tail to bottom of Body between rnds 14 and 18.

Spikes

Note: *Do not stuff Spikes.*

Tiny Spike
Make 2.

Rnd 1 (RS): With smoky green, form a slip ring, 6 sc in ring. *(6 sts)*

Rnd 2: Sc in each st around. *(6 sts)*

Rnd 3: 2 sc in each st around. *(12 sts)*

Fasten off, leaving a 12-inch tail for sewing. Set aside.

Small Spike
Make 3.

Rnds 1–3: Work as for Tiny Spike.

Rnd 4: Sc in each st around. *(12 sts)*

Rnd 5: [2 sc in next st, sc in next 2 sts] around. *(16 sts)*

Fasten off, leaving a 12-inch tail for sewing. Set aside.

Large Spike
Make 2.

Rnds 1–4: Work as for Small Spike.

Rnd 5: [2 sc in next st, sc in next st] around. *(18 sts)*

Rnd 6: Sc in each st around. *(18 sts)*

Fasten off, leaving a 12-inch tail for sewing. Set aside.

Cap

Note: *Graduation Cap is a nice touch if creating as a graduation gift for any age!*

Top Square
Make 2.

Row 1: With coal, ch 15, hdc in 2nd ch from hook and each ch across, turn. *(14 sts)*

Rows 2–10: Ch 1 *(does not count as a st)*, hdc in each st across, turn. *(14 sts)*

Fasten off. On 1 Square, leave a 24-inch tail for sewing. Sew squares tog around outside edges *(RS and WS do not matter)* to form Top of Cap.

Bottom Circle

With coal and leaving a 16-inch tail for sewing, ch 17, join in first ch to form a ring.

Rnd 1 (RS): Ch 1, hdc in each ch around. *(17 sts)*

Rnd 2: Change to deep sea, sl st in each st around. *(17 sts)*

Fasten off, leaving a 16-inch tail for sewing.

With coal beg tail, **sew** *(see Pattern Notes)* Bottom Circle to center of Top of Cap.

With deep sea ending tail, sew Cap to top of Head at a slight angle.

Finishing

Tassel

Row 1 (RS): With sunsoaked and leaving a 6-inch tail, ch 8, sc in 2nd ch from hook and each ch across. *(7 sts)*

Fasten off, leaving a 6-inch tail. Using tapestry needle, pull both tails through center of Cap from top to inside. Tie tails tog inside cap to secure Tassel.

Fringe

Cut 3 12-inch strands of sunsoaked. Fold 3-strand hank in half to form a lp. Insert hook in end of tassel and pull lp halfway through. Pull Fringe ends through lp and pull tightly to secure. Trim Fringe ends evenly.

Attach Spikes

Sew spikes to back of Body in following order, starting at top: tiny, small, small, large, large, small, tiny.

Fingernails
Work once on each Arm and Leg.

With white and tapestry needle, insert needle into side of Arm/Leg, coming out between rnds 2 and 3 where desired for first *(right)* fingernail. *[Insert needle 2 rnds above where it came out and bring it back out through same st where it came out before *(see image)*] 4 times going in and out of the same 2 sts. Insert needle in same st 2 rnds above where it came out *(fingernail made)*** and bring it back out 2 sts to the left of where it came out before. Rep from * for 2nd fingernail, then rep from * to ** for last fingernail, bring needle back out in same st as starting tail. Cut yarn leaving a 5-inch tail. Tie tails tog and tuck into Arm/Leg. ●

Todd the Turtle

Skill Level
Intermediate

Finished Measurement
31 inches long, including hat

Materials
- Bernat Blanket Yarn super bulky (super chunky) weight polyester yarn (10½ oz/220 yds/300g per skein):
    - 1 skein each #10801 aquatic, #10825 dark teal, #10918 sunsoaked and #10630 pumpkin spice
- Bernat Super Value medium (worsted) weight acrylic yarn (7 oz/440 yds/197g per skein):
    - 1 yd each #07391 white and #07421 black (for eyes)
- Size K/10½/6.5mm crochet hook or size needed to obtain gauge
- Tapestry needle
- Fiberfill
- 20mm safety eyes: 2
- Stitch marker

Gauge
With super bulky yarn: 10 dc = 4 inches; 5 dc rnds = 4 inches

Pattern Notes
All pieces begin with a slip ring. If preferred, instead of a slip ring, chain 3 and slip stitch into first chain to form beginning ring.

Do not join or turn at end of rounds unless indicated. Mark first stitch of round and move marker up with each round.

Join with a slip stitch as indicated unless otherwise stated.

Weave in ends as work progresses.

Change colors as indicated by using new color to complete last pull-through step of last stitch of previous color.

Right and left are as you are looking at work throughout. For example, if you are looking at front of Face, right eye is on right as you see it *(which would be Todd's left eye).*

Sew pieces together as indicated with tapestry needle and matching yarn using photos as a guide. Use long tails for sewing wherever possible.

This is a snuggler design, meaning Shell and Tail will not be stuffed.

To embroider eyes in lieu of using safety eyes, see Embroidering Eyes on Amigurumi tutorial on page 2.

Chain-2 at beginning of rounds does not count as a stitch unless otherwise stated.

About Todd

Today is a special day for Todd the Turtle—he is turning 7! Excitement fills his heart as he gets ready for his birthday bash at the local skating rink in Apex, North Carolina. Todd's best friends—Caleb, Elise and Michael—just arrived at his house so they can get ready together. Todd can't wait to glide across the rink with his friends and indulge in pizza, games and cake. His parents planned everything to the smallest detail to ensure Todd has the most memorable birthday. Happy birthday, Todd!

Todd the Turtle

Head

Rnd 1 (RS): With aquatic, form a **slip ring** *(see illustration and Pattern Notes)*, 8 sc in ring, **do not join** *(see Pattern Notes)*. *(8 sts)*

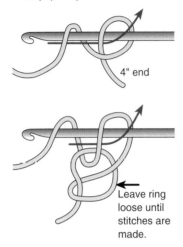

Slip Ring

Leave ring loose until stitches are made.

4" end

Rnd 2: 2 sc in each st around. *(16 sts)*

Rnd 3: [2 sc in next st, sc in next st] around. *(24 sts)*

Rnd 4: [2 sc in next st, sc in next 2 sts] around. *(32 sts)*

Rnd 5: [2 sc in next st, sc in next 3 sts] around. *(40 sts)*

Rnds 6–16: Sc in each st around. *(40 sts)*

Snap in **safety eyes** *(see Pattern Notes)* between rnds 11 and 12 with 2 sts between eyes.

Begin stuffing Head with fiberfill and continue stuffing as work progresses.

Rnd 17: [Sc dec *(see Stitch Guide)* in next 2 sts, sc in next 3 sts] around. *(32 sts)*

Rnd 18: Sc in each st around. *(32 sts)*

Rnd 19: [Sc dec in next 2 sts, sc in next 2 sts] around. *(24 sts)*

Rnd 20: [Sc dec in next 2 sts, sc in next st] around. *(16 sts)*

Rnds 21–24: Sc in each st around. *(16 sts)*

Rnd 25: [Sc dec in next 2 sts, sc in next 2 sts] around, **change to dark teal** *(see Pattern Notes)*. *(12 sts)*

Rnd 26: Sc in each st around. *(12 sts)*

Rnd 27: Sc in each st around. *(12 sts)*

Fasten off, leaving a 12-inch tail for sewing.

Eyebrows

With black and tapestry needle, insert needle into **right** *(see Pattern Notes)* side of head and bring it out between rnds 9 and 10 and in line with right side of right eye, leaving a 5-inch tail. Insert needle 2 sts to left of where it came out and between rnds 7 and 8 *(first eyebrow made)* and bring it out on same row in line with right edge of left eye *(see image)*. Insert needle 2 sts to left of where it came out and between rnds 9 and 10 *(2nd eyebrow made)* and bring it out in same st as beg tail. Cut yarn leaving a 5-inch tail. Tie tails tog and tuck into Head.

Eye Highlights

With white and tapestry needle, insert needle into right side of head and bring it out at top right corner of right eye, leaving a 5-inch tail. Insert needle at bottom center of right eye (*first highlight made*) and bring it out at top left corner of left eye. Insert needle at bottom center of left eye (*2nd highlight made—see image*) and bring it out at same st as beg tail. Cut yarn leaving a 5-inch tail. Tie tails tog and tuck into Head.

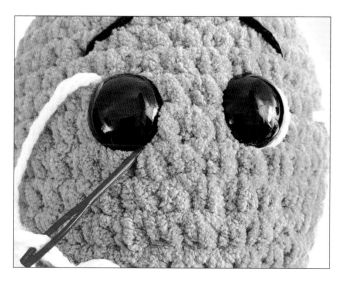

Smile

With black and tapestry needle, insert needle into head between rnds 14 and 15 and aligned with center of right eye and bring it out 3 sts to left, leaving a 5-inch tail. Insert needle into same st as first inserted and come out 1 rnd below and centered between where needle was originally inserted and where it came out (*see image*).

Before tightening st, pass needle under horizontal yarn from bottom to top (*see image*). Insert needle back into same st it just came out of, then bring it out of same st as tail. Cut yarn leaving a 5-inch tail. Tie tails tog and tuck into Head.

Shell

Top of Shell

Rnd 1 (RS): With dark teal, form a slip ring, ch 2, 12 dc in ring, **join** (*see Pattern Notes*) in beg ch-2. (*12 sts*)

Rnd 2: Ch 2, 2 dc in each st around, join in beg ch-2. (*24 sts*)

Rnd 3: Ch 2, 2 dc in first st, dc in next st, [2 dc in next st, dc in next st] around, join in beg ch-2. (*36 sts*)

Rnd 4: Ch 2, 2 dc in first st, dc in next 2 sts, [2 dc in next st, dc in next 2 sts] around, join in beg ch-2. (*48 sts*)

Rnd 5: Ch 2, 2 dc in first st, dc in next 3 sts, [2 dc in next st, dc in next 3 sts] around, join in beg ch-2. (*60 sts*)

Rnd 6: Ch 2, 2 dc in first st, dc in next 4 sts, [2 dc in next st, dc in next 4 sts] around, join in beg ch-2. (*72 sts*)

Rnd 7: Ch 2, 2 dc in first st, dc in next 5 sts, [2 dc in next st, dc in next 5 sts] around, join in beg ch-2. (*84 sts*)

Rnd 8: Ch 2, 2 dc in first st, dc in next 6 sts, [2 dc in next st, dc in next 6 sts] around, join in beg ch-2. *(96 sts)*

Rnds 9 & 10: Ch 2, dc in each st around, join in beg ch-2. *(96 sts)*

Rnd 11: Ch 2, hdc in each st around, join in beg ch-2. *(96 sts)*

Rnd 12: Ch 1, sc in each st around, join in beg ch-2. Fasten off. *(96 sts)*

Bottom of Shell

Rnd 1: Turn shell over to work on inside *(WS)*. With dark teal, working around posts of sts of rnd 9 and inserting hook from front to back and to front again *(see image)*, insert hook in any st, yo and pull up a lp, ch 2, dc in each st around, join in beg ch-2. *(96 sts)*

Rnd 2: Ch 2, **dc dec** *(see Stitch Guide)* in first 2 sts, dc in next 6 sts, [dc dec in next 2 sts, dc in next 6 sts] around, join in beg ch-2. *(84 sts)*

Rnd 3: Ch 2, dc dec in first 2 sts, dc in next 5 sts, [dc dec in next 2 sts, dc in next 5 sts] around, join in beg ch-2. *(72 sts)*

Rnd 4: Ch 2, dc dec in first 2 sts, dc in next 4 sts, [dc dec in next 2 sts, dc in next 4 sts] around, join in beg ch-2. *(60 sts)*

Rnd 5: Ch 2, dc dec in first 2 sts, dc in next 3 sts, [dc dec in next 2 sts, dc in next 3 sts] around, join in beg ch-2. *(48 sts)*

Rnd 6: Ch 2, dc dec in first 2 sts, dc in next 2 sts, [dc dec in next 2 sts, dc in next 2 sts] around, join in beg ch-2. *(36 sts)*

Rnd 7: Ch 2, dc dec in first 2 sts, dc in next st, [dc dec in next 2 sts, dc in next st] around, join in beg ch-2. *(24 sts)*

Rnd 8: Ch 2, dc dec in first 2 sts, [dc dec in next 2 sts] around, join in beg ch-2. *(12 sts)*

Rnd 9: Rep rnd 8. Fasten off. *(6 sts)*

Leg

Make 4.

Rnds 1–4: With aquatic, work as for rnds 1–4 of Head. *(32 sts)*

Rnd 5: Working in **horizontal bar of hdc** *(see illustration)*, sc in each st around. *(32 sts)*

**Horizontal Bar of
Half Double Crochet**

Rnd 6: Working in both lps, sc in each st around. *(32 sts)*

Rnd 7: [Sc dec in next 2 sts, sc in next 2 sts] around. *(24 sts)*

Rnd 8: Sc in each st around. *(24 sts)*

Rnd 9: [Sc dec in next 2 sts, sc in next st] around. *(16 sts)*

Rnds 10–12: Sc in each st around. *(16 sts)*

Rnd 13: [Sc dec in next 2 sts, sc in next st] around. *(12 sts)*

Rnd 14: Sc in each st around. *(12 sts)*

Stuff with fiberfill through rnd 14 only. Do not continue stuffing as work progresses.

Rnd 15: [Sc dec in next 2 sts, sc in next st] around, change to dark teal. *(9 sts)*

Rnd 16: Sc in each st around. *(9 sts)*

Rnd 17: Sc in each st around. *(9 sts)*

Fasten off, leaving a 12-inch tail for sewing.

Tail

Rnd 1: With aquatic, form a slip ring, 6 sc in ring. *(6 sts)*

Rnd 2: Sc in each st around. *(6 sts)*

Rnd 3: 2 sc in each st around. *(12 sts)*

Rnd 4: Sc in each st around. *(12 sts)*

Rnd 5: [2 sc in next st, sc in next st] around. *(18 sts)*

Rnd 6: Sc in each st around, change to dark teal. *(18 sts)*

Rnd 7: Sc in each st around. *(18 sts)*

Fasten off, leaving a 12-inch tail for sewing.

Birthday Hat

Rnd 1: With pumpkin spice, form a slip ring, 8 sc in ring. *(8 sts)*

Rnds 2 & 3: Sc in each st around. *(8 sts)*

Rnd 4: Sc dec in next 2 sts around, change to sunsoaked. *(4 sts)*

Rnd 5: 2 sc in each st around. *(8 sts)*

Rnd 6: Sc in each st around. *(8 sts)*

Rnd 7: 2 dc in each st around. *(16 sts)*

Rnds 8 & 9: Sc in each st around. *(16 sts)*

Rnd 10: 2 dc in first st, sc in next 3 sts, [2 dc in next st, sc in next 3 sts] around. *(20 sts)*

Rnds 11–14: Sc in each st around, change to pumpkin spice. *(20 sts)*

Rnd 15: 2 dc in first st, sc in next 4 sts, [2 dc in next st, sc in next 4 sts] around, change to aquatic. *(24 sts)*

Rnd 16: Sl st in each st around.

Fasten off, leaving a 16-inch tail for sewing.

Assembly

Turn Shell upside down with Bottom of Shell facing up. **Sew** *(see Pattern Notes)* rnds 26 and 27 of Head to WS of rnds 10 and 11 of Top of Shell.

Sew rnds 16 and 17 of 2 Legs to Bottom of Shell along rnds 1–3 and centered across Head.

Sew rnds 16 and 17 of rem 2 Legs to Bottom of Shell along rnds 5–7 and directly above previously sewn Legs.

Sew Tail to rnd 11 of Top of Shell, centered between Legs.

Sew Birthday Hat to head at an angle between rnds 1 and 8. ●

STITCH GUIDE

STITCH ABBREVIATIONS

beg .... begin/begins/beginning
bpdc .... back post double crochet
bpsc .... back post single crochet
bptr .... back post treble crochet
CC .... contrasting color
ch(s) .... chain(s)
ch- .... refers to chain or space
           previously made (i.e., ch-1 space)
ch sp(s) .... chain space(s)
cl(s) .... cluster(s)
cm .... centimeter(s)
dc .... double crochet (singular/plural)
dc dec .... double crochet 2 or more
           stitches together, as indicated
dec .... decrease/decreases/decreasing
dtr .... double treble crochet
ext .... extended
fpdc .... front post double crochet
fpsc .... front post single crochet
fptr .... front post treble crochet
g .... gram(s)
hdc .... half double crochet
hdc dec .... half double crochet 2 or more
           stitches together, as indicated
inc .... increase/increases/increasing
lp(s) .... loop(s)
MC .... main color
mm .... millimeter(s)
oz .... ounce(s)
pc .... popcorn(s)
rem .... remain/remains/remaining
rep(s) .... repeat(s)
rnd(s) .... round(s)
RS .... right side(s)
sc .... single crochet (singular/plural)
sc dec .... single crochet 2 or more
           stitches together, as indicated
sk .... skip/skipped/skipping
sl st(s) .... slip stitch(es)
sp(s) .... space(s)/spaced
st(s) .... stitch(es)
tog .... together
tr .... treble crochet
trtr .... triple treble
WS .... wrong side(s)
yd(s) .... yard(s)
yo .... yarn over

YARN CONVERSION

OUNCES TO GRAMS		GRAMS TO OUNCES	
1	28.4	25	⅞
2	56.7	40	1⅔
3	85.0	50	1¾
4	113.4	100	3½

UNITED STATES		UNITED KINGDOM
sl st (slip stitch)	=	sc (single crochet)
sc (single crochet)	=	dc (double crochet)
hdc (half double crochet)	=	htr (half treble crochet)
dc (double crochet)	=	tr (treble crochet)
tr (treble crochet)	=	dtr (double treble crochet)
dtr (double treble crochet)	=	ttr (triple treble crochet)
skip	=	miss

Reverse single crochet (reverse sc): Ch 1, sk first st, working from left to right, insert hook in next st from front to back, draw up lp on hook, yo and draw through both lps on hook.

Chain (ch): Yo, pull through lp on hook.

Single crochet (sc): Insert hook in st, yo, pull through st, yo, pull through both lps on hook.

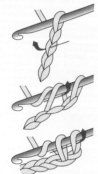

Double crochet (dc): Yo, insert hook in st, yo, pull through st, [yo, pull through 2 lps] twice.

Single crochet decrease (sc dec): (Insert hook, yo, draw lp through) in each of the sts indicated, yo, draw through all lps on hook.

Example of 2-sc dec

Half double crochet decrease (hdc dec): (Yo, insert hook, yo, draw lp through) in each of the sts indicated, yo, draw through all lps on hook.

Example of 2-hdc dec

Front loop (front lp): Back loop (back lp):

Front Loop   Back Loop

Front post stitch (fp): Back post stitch (bp): When working post st, insert hook from right to left around post of st on previous row.

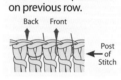

Back   Front

Post of Stitch

Half double crochet (hdc): Yo, insert hook in st, yo, pull through st, yo, pull through all 3 lps on hook.

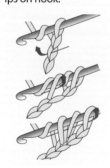

Double treble crochet (dtr): Yo 3 times, insert hook in st, yo, pull through st, [yo, pull through 2 lps] 4 times.

Double crochet decrease (dc dec): (Yo, insert hook, yo, draw lp through, yo, draw through 2 lps on hook) in each of the sts indicated, yo, draw through all lps on hook.

Example of 2-dc dec

Slip stitch (sl st): Insert hook in st, pull through both lps on hook.

Chain color change (ch color change): Yo with new color, draw through last lp on hook.

Double crochet color change (dc color change): Drop first color, yo with new color, draw through last 2 lps of st.

Treble crochet (tr): Yo twice, insert hook in st, yo, pull through st, [yo, pull through 2 lps] 3 times.

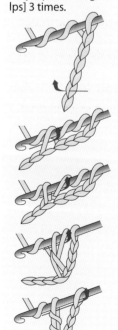

Treble crochet decrease (tr dec): Holding back last lp of each st, tr in each of the sts indicated, yo, pull through all lps on hook.

Example of 2-tr dec

47

Meet the Designer

Marcy Wynn Gardner

Marcy is the amigurumi designer behind Simply Hooked crochet patterns. She learned how to crochet in 2012, quickly fell in love with the craft and has been perfecting it ever since. Designing amigurumi is her favorite creative outlet.

Marcy is passionate about the art of crochet and enjoys writing patterns that are beginner-friendly so crocheters of any level have an enjoyable crafting experience. She resides in North Carolina with her family.

🌐 **Website:** www.marcymade.co

📷 **Instagram:** @SimplyHooked1

📘 **Facebook:** @SimplyHooked1

Annie's® Published by Annie's, 306 East Parr Road, Berne, IN 46711. Printed in USA. Copyright © 2025 Annie's. All rights reserved. This publication may not be reproduced in part or in whole without written permission from the publisher.

RETAIL STORES: If you would like to carry this publication or any other Annie's publication, visit AnniesWSL.com.

Every effort has been made to ensure that the instructions in this publication are complete and accurate. We cannot, however, take responsibility for human error, typographical mistakes or variations in individual work. Please visit AnniesCustomerService.com to check for pattern updates.

ISBN: 979-8-89253-389-8

1 2 3 4 5 6 7 8 9